The Ars Magna for the Manifold Dimensions of z

Don't read this book if you're looking for easy answers. Or perhaps any answers. Don't read this book if you enjoy and/or need a book that is logical in any way because "Logic is a form of treason, my furry friend." So don't read this book if you are a non-furry friend. Or a furry enemy. Don't even think about reading this book if you are not occasionally stuck in an elevator or in love. Do read this book if you enjoy Borges or Vonnegut, among others, maybe even De la Flor's previous books, like *Sinead O'Connor and Her Coat of a Thousand Bluebirds*, written during his Metalingual Miami Period with a starfish named Star Fish. Do read this book if you think life is same old or if the way you tie knots has got you down. This book is a trip. Take it or not, it's up to you. It's possibly a real book, after all. ("This space is intentionally left speechless.") Ask yourself: "Will a pickle hold you over, my dear?" If the answer is yes, or especially if it's no, read this book. I did.

—Maureen Seaton, author of *Metablurbs & Mudlarks*

Also by Neil de la Flor

An Elephant's Memory of Blizzards (2013)

Almost Dorothy (2010)

Collaborative Works

Reading Queer: Poetry in a Time of Chaos (2018) co-edited with Maureen Seaton

Two Thieves & a Liar (2012) co-authored with Maureen Seaton and Kristine Snodgrass

Sinéad O'Connor and her Coat of a Thousand Bluebirds (2011) co-authored with Maureen Seaton

Facial Geometry (2006) co-authored with Maureen Seaton and Kristine Snodgrass

The Ars Magna for the Manifold Dimensions of z

Neil de la Flor

JACKLEG PRESS

For more information on this book or to order, visit
www.jacklegpress.org

To learn more about Neil de la Flor, please visit his
website: www.neildelaflor.com

Published by

JackLeg Press
Washington, DC

ISBN: 978-1-7373307-4-5

Library of Congress Cataloging-in-Publication Data

Cover design by Richard Every.
Cover art "Brine" by Jean-Paul Mallozzi.

Contents

"For most non-Jewish Danish prisoners, the period between their arrest and their arrival at a concentration camp was often more traumatic than the actual camp experience. Prisoners suspected of resistance work were subjected to solitary confinement, interrogation, and torture. Death and permanent impairment followed, even if they were subjected to no further hardships in the camp."

—Richard Petrow, *The Bitter Years*

Prologue

Meta was driving west on Sheridan Street when a drunk driver collided with her Chrysler LeBaron Town & Country station wagon. He drove a white pickup truck that was (heading) northbound on North 66th Avenue just east of University Drive. Meta was on her way home from Jai-Alai. It was July 1990. The day before the accident, Meta began to reveal secrets over California rolls and iced tea at Nami's.

Ø

On April 9th, 1940, the Nazi regime invaded Denmark. Meta, along with her husband, infant son, brother, other family members, and most of the Danish people, joined and/or actively supported the Danish Underground Resistance. One day the Gestapo captured Meta, her husband, and several of her family members, and charged them with sabotage. They killed her son. They tortured and killed her husband, too. Meta didn't have a chance to swallow the pill.

Ø

Meta and her sister, Lilly, survived the concentration camps, but the "examination" before their departure split Meta into two. The Gestapo may have tied her legs and arms to a hook on a wall; they may have tied her legs and arms to a pallet; they may not have bothered to tie her up at all; they may have pummeled her sex organs with rubber blackjacks; they may have penetrated her sex organs with rubber blackjacks; they may have just used the raw beastly power of their hairy fists. There is no record of this, but Meta's hair never grew back, and she could never bear children again.

Ø

After the war, Meta met The American, a rancorous army cook. They met on Sunday, married on Wednesday, and moved to Jersey City where they bought a diner that burned down in a fire a year later. It was 1946. Before they moved to Florida, Meta and The American adopted a baby girl on February 5th, 1949. They named her Lillian.

Ø

Lillian came into this world on February 5th, 1949, at Margaret Hague Hospital in Hudson County, New

Jersey. Meta and The American adopted her at two days old. When Lillian was born, she had spinal meningitis, and was in the hospital for a couple of weeks. Lillian grew up in Jersey City and went to a Catholic School. She was always afraid of the nuns and their love of the paddle and the whip.

Ø

Meta is so many different things. She is a prefix. She is intended for those things that are meta to mud. Meta is 't'ime. She is an organization of humane volunteers. She is completely voluntary. She signifies the close relationship that minerals have with their cousins. She is stable. She is a hard worker, and she loves to gamble. She is the exception. She is the object that describes other objects. Meta is already in the results. She is not quick to explain, but she is an individual living somewhere in the world. Meta is the data note that all metadata is.

Ø

It was Friday, July 13, 1990, when The American called Lillian about the accident. They went to the hospital together. There is no complete record of Meta or her participation in the Danish Underground Resistance. This is the only record that exists.

Part 1 | Meta

"And while the Boy was asleep, dreaming of the seaside, the little Rabbit lay among the old picture-books in the corner behind the fowl-house, and he felt very lonely. The sack had been left untied, and so by wriggling a bit he was able to get his head through the opening and look out."

— Margery Williams,
The Velveteen Rabbit

Minkowskian Spacetime: The Geometry of Meta

"Home is pure concept, not reality"

—Patrick Friesen

On Black Friday Meta and I bought matching pink barrettes and Pepperidge Farm Goldfish Crackers because it was the stupidest thing we could do with two bucks. When we walked out of K-mart, we looked like two freaks dancing to the "Neutron Dance" in our heads. I had long hair then, strawberry cheeks, and people just stared at our wits. That's when Meta morphed into Marilyn Monroe. Meta was less attractive than MM, but that didn't matter. She was the fattest thing I remember about 1984 [besides Ryan White]. *Watch this*, she said, and then gave them the finger.

Ø

The "I" of this story is not "me." [The "I" may be "z," or "negative z," or a mutation and recombination zs, who are not the children of kangaroos or gods, but are possibly the children of kangaroo gods.] They are plurals, not deficits. Multiple drafts of consciousness. The "I" may be manifold [dimensions of z], or spatial geometries that depend on one another to exist. Or, the "I" may simply be the space that exists between the stars where z and -z occupy the space between Meta and me.

$$\varnothing$$

The next act is bizarre, patience isn't a virtue, and I won't make it painless: z is the boy looking for answers, an archivist of sorts, a kite without a string looking for strings from an Internet cafe on Miami Beach. The Boy is the boy looking for z. Both are mirror images of each other and are obsessed with mathematics, specifically infinite geometry. For example, if z were to take the place of the real-number system, in any significant case, then the *Boy* would have to be very large so that '$z+z+...+z=0$' would not show a serious discrepancy in observed behavior. The two boys are bound to Meta, unrelated to one another, but "I" hold the barrettes.

$$\varnothing$$

When inappropriate, Meta would sound like a trucker to give her more credibility in public spaces. She once peed on the floor at McDonald's because the manager would only allow customers to take a leak. Meta was not afraid of consequences or humiliation. She would have been Nan Goldin, or one of the subjects of Nan's art, such as the woman being embraced in "The Hug."

Ø

Meta met The American in Denmark while he was serving overseas after the war was won. Fortunately for them, they practiced oral sex. *At all times,* she said, which meant they didn't have sex, but kissed heavily and heavy petted, which is—according to Meta—the best sex there is, except for head. *It's kind of like a Big Mac without the meat,* she said.

Ø

[When they ate, they made love.]

He said: I want to tie you up.
            I want to eat you like a chicken.
            I want to zigzag down your back until

you're mine.

She said: I want to be scrumptious.
                I want to know Methuselah's secret.
                I want to copyright my favorite genes.

Ø

The crowd [meaning you, dear reader, or the person reading over your shoulder] by now must be restless for a simple linear narrative that documents Meta's revelations over sushi on that fateful day, but keep in mind, you are invisible to both z and the Boy. They are observing you from above and are not concerned if you are unimpressed and bored with what you've heard so far. [They do care about you.] Imagine you are now inside an opera house inside of a tambourine [trust me] and thrust your head around until you see Meta's giant well-coiffed poodles [if you squint] guard a semi-grand foyer. They are invisible to no one, not even the blind. The usher guarding orchestra right is radiating an electromagnetic field, sort of, under her black & gray streaked wig. She is utterly enthralled by the performance because this is her first gig as a volunteer human. She knows that this experience beats sitting on the porch of her one-story gentrified cottage. *It's all around you*, the human usher shouts to the customers

4

as if they're unaware that they are inside and out.

Ø

When I contacted the National Archives in Copenhagen, or Rigsarkivet, the guardian of the Danish archives resisted my call for information and such. They said, in Danish, Meta didn't exist. *But she did*, I said, *I swear. I still have her wigs and her pink barrettes.* I thought part of me would speak Danish and reveal secrets to the other part of me. In sonar perhaps.

Ø

I know. I am going back and forth for no reason at all. The fact that I went back and forth to Denmark and returned without a shred of evidence of Meta's existence, or z's, or -z's, or Meta's first husband, doesn't mean I'm sitting on my porch, thumbless. I went over and over and over it again with the staff but to no avail. They treated me like an Ugly Duckling dress. *The Rigsarkivet*, they said, *is not for wimps.*

Ø

Meta took me to Las Vegas on Eastern Airlines. She dressed up as Cher, and I dressed up as Sonny as the Rhinestone Cowboy. That's when we ran into the real [or "real"] Sonny & Cher on The Strip. Our idol mirrors. Neither of us knew what each of us felt at that moment. Star struck or shot down, perhaps, because we were not the center of the universe anymore—we were just two brown fish in the Pacific who refused to think of the consequences of dressing up in public. We refueled on Root Beer floats. We had to pee so bad that we left The Strip for the all you can eat buffet at Harrah's [restroom]. We decided then and somewhat there that the chance meeting of these legends in Las Vegas meant that we were holy again. We huddled together in our all get-out crouching beneath the entrance to the Starlight Express.

Ø

My boy, she said, *the things you'll fight against are earthquakes compared to this.*

Ø

Meta was clairvoyant too.

Ø

On Sundays, Meta and I would watch football at the Orange Bowl. She'd order me a hot dog and call me a wiener with mustard on her face. She always called the shots from the 40-yard line. I had no idea which tight end did what, but it didn't matter. I screamed at him anyway. When overtime ended, we walked around for a while because we couldn't find where she parked the wagon. *Come on*, Meta said. *I don't have all night.*

Ø

She wore sandstone for a woman who had not grown for years. Unable to fetch Frisbees in winter lodged into clouds, she got fed up with seahorses. Her manuscript uttered not a word about white busses with red crosses. She found miracles in minor miracles, acted like a magician without a hat. *If my head had been cut off,* she said, *you would've been next.*

Ø

Meta: You seem to have gone overboard with this. [As if the dead can speak to the living, or vice versa, and that's when I decided to uncover Meta's psychosis years before I knew how to spell it]. Meta: Your responses are manic at best. Breakneck and full of dust. [I spent evenings researching at 56k between sewing evening dresses for clients. The clogged artery opened new dimensions for me.] Meta: When you logged off Rigsarkivet, you found the lost geometry of z in a photo album with sepia prints in Lillian's basement. [See: photographs.] Meta: Please, boy, (pause 3 seconds) confess your stones and spaceships to the wind. [I never went to Rigsarkivet.] Meta: You couldn't afford the roundtrip plane ticket across the Atlantic. [The rest is ancient history.]

Ø

As I said before [or will say in the future] there was an artifact of sorts, a tiny boy-craft perhaps, a small boat for fishing, a z and a negative z, a flick of the wrist, an archivist with chains and whips, a war and a wicked witch. Pink barrettes and K-mart trips. Even Vlasic pickles for snacks. Well, there wasn't a witch, but there were wolves and a concentration camp where Meta did women's work and lost her grip—

Ø

in Frøslev.

Frøslev

"The Frøslev Camp was built as a German internment camp in 1944 during the German occupation of Denmark and is one of Europe's most well preserved German camps from World War II. Several thousand Danes were imprisoned by the German security police (Gestapo) in the Frøslev Camp. Even though the Frøslev Camp was built to avoid the deportation of Danes to concentration camps in Germany, some 1.600 Frøslev prisoners were in fact deported to the horrors of these camps."

—Nationalmuseet,
National Museum of Denmark

Meta hustled in a soup kitchen full of children and small men disguised as women disguised as weapons. Children wore aprons with enormous dimensions as they hung upside down by their toes just because or just in case someone Achooed. Meta counted the fleas in her bed day after day.

Meta: We were smashed together—sardine-like and salty. For the hell of it. I painted the sky with imaginary pigment. The daily bread just fit in the tip of my shoes.

It took a while to adjust to push up bras
in the 50s, but when I got out of the camp,
I used them to summon arthropods on
the weekend.

Ø

My Boy, she said. Swear off helicopters. Always tiptoe
on the ledge of disaster.

Ø

A week before Thanksgiving Meta wouldn't lay off the
algebraic equations:

$$\sqrt[3]{-\frac{q}{2} + \sqrt{\frac{q^2}{4} + \frac{p^3}{27}}} + \sqrt[3]{-\frac{q}{2} - \sqrt{\frac{q^2}{4} + \frac{p^3}{27}}},$$

q, she said, equals the sum of my ancestors.

p, she said, equals antipasto, which is like the ancestor
you never wanted, but have, like uncles.

You better learn your p's and q's, she said, because you

never know where you'll land.

Ø

Meta never knew what hit her. She never knew I stopped going to the Orange Bowl and no longer shop at K-mart. She never knew I became the archivist of sorts. She never knew I'd grow up to be gay or temporarily gothic. I'm somewhat ridiculous without her these days. She never knew I wanted to know more about her magic shoes and the stuff that made them move after her stint in the camp. She never knew the complex nature of Minkowskian Spacetime or what comforts inanimate objects in a vacuum.

Ø

[Excerpt from the final act:] The crowd is utterly complex and seated on the edge of their seats while the stagehand is on stage as stationary as ever before, and exquisitely staged. For no reason at all the giant well-coiffed poodles begin to chant, or om, or make sounds that are somewhat chant-like and ommish. They bark in sequence. The audience leans in [stupefied, I guess] as if the one and only Judy Garland emerges from behind the gates of Oz, but it is not Judy Garland per se, nor Liza in drag, but Meta before she fled with The American to America. She is [Meta] dressed in black and swaddles the small boy tight. She then lifts his lifeless body to the gods and goddesses of stage and screen and places him upstage. In real-time, she wears an auburn wig with relaxed curls (that I updated to fit this narrative). The Jai-Alai players begin a round robin of whispers.

All stop.

Meta: Bones of goldfish, archive the past.

Ø

So, I did. This is [more or less] what happened: Meta shuttled Jews across the arctic; she didn't shuttle Jews across the arctic; there's no archive of this in Rigsarkivet, but there are ancestors; there are eggs & spermatozoa; she was a klutz; she peed a lot; enjoyed sex incognito and wore sexy lingerie; distributed glossy propaganda against the occupiers while she was occupied herself with the impossible pregnancy of z; she was a collaborator; she was not a traitor; she was a traitor; she never collaborated with traitors; she buried her boy in secret; in shame; there were no secrets; shame followed her husband to the ledge of disaster, but stepped back; she jumped in; she didn't jump; she buried the revolver in the sky; she buried the boy in the sky; buried the sky in the boy; she traded bees for honey; honed her hunting skills; played helmsman/woman of fishing boats; scrubbed boat decks with remarkable precision; five finger discounted; threatened football players with pistols and whips; whipped ass; played mouse; never kissed on the mouth again.

Ø

When I was a kid, our favorite dance was the hula.

Part 2 | The Archivists

"Oarsman, oarsman
  What did you there?
I hid in a cleft,
I braided the air."

—Susan Howe

The Archivists

"If the Germans want to introduce the Yellow Star for Jews in Denmark, I and my whole family will wear it as a sign of the highest distinction."

—falsely attributed to
King Christian X of Denmark

Act 1, Scene 1

[The arctic is up and downstage. Two small boys row center stage in a rowboat and wear matching navy blue pea coats buttoned up over white overall jumpers. They are approximately 6 years old, the boys, not the jumpers, and they are indistinguishable from one another. The pink barrette in their hair is almost visible to the audience. The spotlight diffuses through a dense fog.]

z & -z: Is there an artifact that spans the
            Atlantic, a genetic offspring of sorts?

z & -z: Well, of course there is silly, you're
            talking to him right now, that offspring
            of sorts.

z & -z: What was your source?

z & -z: She was the source, of course.

z & -z: She, meaning, who?

z & -z: By she I mean the girl who learned to
             scrub in protest before the invention of
             the Magic Eraser and the Swiffer. The
             photographs she left me have been
             Xeroxed into memory with much
             precision, in sepia, I swear.

[The projector projects sepia photographs against the
dense fog.]

z & -z: She said the power of fishing boats is
             remarkable in winter, but not as
             remarkable as a one-night stand on the
             stage of war.

z & -z: Is it safe to say she was not opposed to
             sex during the war?

z & -z: It is, but that's not the point.

z & -z: Then, who is she?

z & -z: She is the progenitor of all this, the

algebraic equation that equals the sum
of my bones.

z & -z: And the sum equals?

z & -z: The scattered bones of our ancestors.

z & -z: How were her bones scattered about?

z & -z: The wind! The wind!

[The wind machine doesn't turn on. Don't even think
about it.]

z & -z: A Nordic wind?

z & -z: No, but a cold tempest that equaled six
               million breaths.

[The audience exhales without a fuss. A woman gasps
from the orchestra left.]

z & -z: Her bones passed through the streets in
               silence as howling women howled at the
               Gestapo who cracked the bones of the
               demonstrators in the underground
               strongholds of Copenhagen. With pitch-
               forked cries of 'Down with the traitors'
               and 'God save the kind kind king' the

demonstrators were promptly kaput by the black boots in charge.

z & -z: And then?

z & -z: She said she swept the bloody streets and hummed la la la and ba ba do. She unplanned her escape with the little boy who she planned to have nestled in her tummy for all eternity. She understood the rush of sex in dark alleys for the first time and prostituted lullabies for money.

z & -z: Was she a prostitute?

z & -z: Of another kind.

z & -z: I'm not sure that I understand where you are headed with this.

z & -z: It takes time, my kind friend.

z & -z: And nuts and wisdom.

z & -z: So, then what? This is wisdom?

z & -z: No. But tanks.

z & -z: The what? The tanks?

z & -z: In unison, scores of protesters were run
            down by tanks, Winnie-the-Poohed out
            of existence in front of her eyes.

[A small boy emerges from the dense fog and drags a
tattered semi-plush Winnie the Pooh across the stage,
which is staged as the arctic. He wears a white overall
jumper with thin blue stripes and white suspenders.
The boy exits stage left. He is approximately 3 years
old. The director may cut this stage direction, but
don't. The boy is a girl dressed as a boy. It will work
out in the end. Perhaps.]

z & -z: Why?

z & -z: No notes on this, but across the road she
            escaped into an antique bookshop with
            the small boy by her side. He dragged a
            stuffed bear by his side. The bear
            dragged what was left of history. He
            was the boy that she buried who she
            would later refer to as ancient history.

z & -z: He was her entire language of sorts, a
            kind of fleshy gobbledygook of tiny
            enormity.

z & -z: Did he like to read?

z & -z: The kind boy always found solace in
           books—preferably Nordic tales of
           conquest and lust. He, with her by his
           side, begged her for an army of winged
           horses to fly them out of the ionosphere,
           the anti-Icarus of sorts. He was ignorant
           of maps and the danger of cumulus
           nimbuses. He swallowed books whole.

z & -z: And then—

z & -z: In her limited wisdom, she smacked
           him.

z & -z: That doesn't make any sense. Are you
           an idiot?

z & -z: Logic is a form of treason, my furry
           friend.

z & -z: And what of treason?

z & -z: No comment beyond it's a form of
           ransom to logic.

z & -z: And what of their fate, of the boy and
           his mother. Are they fairies or friends?

[The projector projects a documentary film against the dense fog as the rest of the scene unfolds. The film opens with Meta sitting on a large rock propping up the boy. She wears a gorgeous spring dress while she makes a Pact of Resistance with the kind boy, a simple smile and a frown the only clue to their secret plan. She is about to cross her legs and wink-wink with her left eye when the film cuts and then loops. The boy is approximately 1 - 2 years old. z & -z stop rowing.]

z & -z: And, bam! It is done. Voilà. The kind King had spoken of this. The boy would spend time with the underground resistance, and so she began to dig and dig and dig until she struck oil or something that approximates heaven.

z & -z: What is the point that you want to make?

z & -z: I do not know.

z & -z: It is hard for me to believe you especially since you are not of Nordic descent, nor do I get the sense you're telling the truth, or care to have your facts verified. It's in my gut, this feeling I have for you.

z & -z: Here's a bit of evidence.

[z hands -z a photograph of Meta and The Boy while -z hands z the same photograph of Meta and The Boy.]

z & -z: I don't believe this is you.

z & -z: It is not. It's them. His feet are too small for wings.

z & -z: Like a footprint.

z & -z: Or a holograph.

z & -z: What if the war did not end?

z & -z: Then you would not exist. She would've worn red socks for Christmas, offered striking workers a shot of whisky, and contemplated the possibility of extramarital sex.

z & -z: And of the boy. What happened to him?

z & -z: She tossed his bones to the wind, and then some. He had no choice and no concept of flight.

z & -z: Why did she do this to him?

z & -z: So that he would be saved.

z & -z: And then?

z & -z: Not all fishing boats reached their final
           destination.

[Their rowboat does not rock or betray the slightest
notion that danger lurks. At this point in the scene, the
documentary film reveals a fleet of wooden fishing
boats skimming near the Danish coast. In the final
scene of the short film, Meta and her sister, Lilly, scrub
their fishing boat.]

z & -z: Some boats ended up under the sea.
           Other boats were set on fire. The wind
           retains a record of all of this.

z & -z: She hid in a cleft.

z & -z: She braided the air.

z & -z: The underground resistance prepared
           eleven fishing boats. Meta's was number
           nine. She almost made it to Sweden.

z & -z: And then?

[The projector projects a short clip of z & -z resetting

the cable connection on their knees.]

z & -z: I am on my knees in the living room
                 resetting the cable connection, and this
                 act reminds me of the image of Meta on
                 her knees scrubbing the fishing boat just
                 before she was captured and sent to the
                 camps—the one where they ended her
                 chances for another kind of offspring.

z & -z: And then?

z & -z: We ended up here in Jersey City, our
                 bones separated by the invisible space
                 between us, the antechamber where all
                 had been done. She never revealed the
                 secret history of the underground
                 resistance, of the boy she left behind, or
                 the woman who gave him up.

[The stage goes black except for the film being
projected against the dense fog. z & -z are nowhere to
be found on stage except for the z & -z in the film being
projected against the dense fog.]

z & -z: Do you often find yourself walking into
                 lamp posts or having sex with
                 strangers?

z & -z: Yes, something like that.

z & -z: But seriously, concerning my question,
               do you believe her story about the boy
               whose bones she chucked to the wind?

z & -z: In retrospect, I believe in magic and the
               power of persuasion. And the flight of
               concords, too.

z & -z: But, in the end?

z & -z: No one was there to catch him when she
               left.

The Ars Magna for the Manifold Dimensions of z

$f(z) = 1/2$

Act 2, Scene 1

[The equation above fades in and fades out against the curtain before it rises and reveals the Danish seaside. Meta and the boy (as z & -z) sit on a large rock. She props the boy up so that he doesn't fall backwards. She wears a gorgeous spring dress. She is about to cross her legs and wink-wink with her left eye, but the wind carries a single grain of sand into her eye. The boy is approximately 1 - 2 years old. Winnie the Pooh is on the grass and is almost invisible to the audience. The lighting is whatever.]

z & -z: If a boy is no longer z, or is negative z, then what is he?

Meta: To heck with z and your negativity, but if you really want to know, then beg.

z & -z: I am, you see? I'm on my knees.

Meta: Well, then, let's begin. If the boy is no
           longer z or is negative z, then he is a
           critter de Profundis. By this I mean,
           well, I'm not sure, but he is definitely no
           longer a boy of this domain space where
           he was once beaten into a holier-than-
           thou manifold, sanctified, classified,
           pick-pocketed, pistol-whipped,
           stereotyped and possibly punched
           choirboy.

z & -z: And then?

Meta: And then, when they were done with
           him, he was made invisible to
           radioscopy where all objects in or on the
           body, such as the cross tattooed on his
           right arm (and plunked on his grave)
           and his heart (tattooed on his chest), are
           destroyed by weathering or landscaping
           or both.

z & -z: By they, you mean, who?

Meta: Those with pistols and whips.

z & -z: I'm still not clear about the whips, but I
           get the sense that the boy is a modern-
           day Gilgamesh?

Meta:	He is not unlike a triptych or an epic sub-text.
z & -z:	If the heart and the cross are removed, or weathered over time, then what is left?
Meta:	An ancestor and a gravitational field, which is like a cosmic macramé, all knotted up but with nowhere to go. In other words, he is like two scoops of your favorite cereal.
z & -z:	Lucky Charms?
Meta:	I suppose.
z & -z:	But, I really don't get you —
Meta:	Neither do I, but you can read lips.
z & -z:	Come close.
Meta:	You see, a boy is a patchwork (or macramé) of basic strings wound up tight to create a new kind of space, a face, arms, and legs. He is a kind of theoretical algebra, but with his own nutty Decalogue, an exquisite corpse

with a severe case of micropsia.

z & -z: I don't get you, ever, you big Pooh!

Meta: Is it time for supper?

z & -z: Let's eat. My belly aches for ham.

Meta: Are you hungry?

z & -z: Yes, but a kiss would suffice. Where do
            secrets come from?

Meta: Kisses and Socrates, I guess, ha-ha, no-
            no. Secrets, and probably Socrates,
            originated from a closed interior kiss,
            i.e., in utero.

z & -z: In the womb?

Meta: Or bomb, or a cul-de-sac void of
            unbearable frictions, i.e., the womb, not
            bomb.

z & -z: Help me untie my sneakers. I need a
            hand.

Meta: What's your thinking process, my friend?
            Knots and knits? Bird brains and kisses?

31

z & -z: You are not a horse, my friend.

Meta: Some will call it a 'grieving' (pause 3 seconds) or a 'lamenting,' but this is reckless, I prefer gambling instead. When shoelaces are tied [imagine a long shot of this and then project it against the backdrop] it takes on a particular significance when all you see are the shoes being tied by almost middle-aged hands.

z & -z: What the heck are middle-aged hands?

Meta: A wicked gnarl of fat cuneiforms.

z & -z: What happens when you squint?

Meta: I get the impression of aliens.

z & -z: Extraterrestrials?

Meta: Yep, you bet.

z & -z: I found this quote on your bureau — "In 3-space (height, width and depth) two half planes meet at an [a]angle-(alpha) along a cosmic string." What does this

32

mean?

Meta: To hell with quotes, my boy. I'm tired of poppycock.

z & -z: To hell with you instead.

Meta: Ok, listen. Let's go for a trip.

z & -z: I am.

Meta: Imagine—

z & -z: That word is so cliché.

Meta: Listen. Imagine—

z & -z: Ok.

Meta: One boy (z) is lost forever to a river while another boy (let's call him negative z) is lost to another river.

z & -z: Ok?

[A silent recording plays, but the audience hears the music in their heads because the director has asked them to play their favorite song in their heads. Do not project a clip of two rivers. Ever.]

Meta: Where these rivers intersect
             (simultaneously in imaginary space and
             real space) you wind-up with a mini
             bang, a kind of 3-dimensional kiss
             between the real boy and the imaginary
             boy, the unification of z and negative z.

z & -z: Makes no sense.

Meta: Nonsense. Imagine that these two boys
             are not the same, but they are identical
             in nature and equal in stature, but only
             in death.

z & -z: This is what it means to be in 3-space
             when your time is up? The boy is dead,
             has drowned in some fashion? The boy
             z and the boy negative z are the same,
             but exist in alternate universes?

Meta: Multiverses, in fact, or in different
             station wagons. Do you believe in
             magic, my boy? Superheroes? Friends?

z & -z: I ask the questions here. Say it in plain
             English.

Meta: This is mathematics and myth, not
             gibberish, my friend.

z & -z: What is mythology to you, my friend?

Meta: A constant fishing, a flick of the wrist,
               the cosmic string.

z & -z: The—what?

Meta: (z) is the boy who travels his entire life
               without the safety of seat belts and
               (negative z) is the deformed, misshapen,
               and haphazard choirboy involved with
               pistols and whips. Do I have to spell it
               out in plain English?

z & -z: Yes.

Meta: He is the result of Zoroastrianism, and
               an ancient battle between pistols and
               whips.

z & -z: I still don't understand.

Meta: Zygotes and spaceships.

z & -z: What—? In the end, so that they may
               understand, what is $f(z) = 1/2$?

[The magical equation is projected against a black
backdrop.]

Meta: f is the magical effect left by stars
             moving through time. (z) was the time
             we moved through the stars. What
             remains equals half of the gravitational
             attraction left by all objects in a room at
             a particular point in time even after
             those objects in the room no longer
             exist.

z & -z: Like the impression we leave on the
             grass after a picnic?

Meta: Sounds loco, but I'd say neither. It's the
             ratio of the distance between the grass
             and the grass before it was flattened by
             our asses.

z & -z: And the boy?

[Meta's tone shifts. She sounds somewhat wiser, and
her voice is deeper, yet softer, almost motherly, yet
fierce and firm, and serious like all get out.]

Meta: He is so much like you.

z & -z: In what way?

[Meta's tone shifts toward the nostalgic, melancholic,
as if it isn't obvious by now.]

Meta: He had a fetish for spelling and
           trinkets—

z & -z: And sneakers and secrets?

Meta: I would have offered you a flotation
           device if I had the wits.

[The audience is now aware that the boy is wearing
adorable sneakers. Couples in the audience look at one
another when they recognize their own offspring in the
story unfolding in front of them.]

z & -z: They were too big for my arms. "You
           cannot swim the length of the Arctic in
           one breath," you said.

Meta;   "I can," you said.

z & -z: I did!

Meta: You did! Now do you understand?

z & -z: All I know is that we meet here again in
           this unholy place confessing our secrets
           to this rock and the wind. We swim
           toward one another in perilous
           synchronicity, fat black tadpoles in full
           regalia, i.e., nada-at-all.

Meta: Between you and me, I hope they will
             understand.

z & -z: Clandestine trips and mathematical b.s.?

Meta: And the boy who was sacrificed for the
             resistance.

z & -z: I won't hold my breath.

Meta: Do you still think about me?

z & -z: Like never before.

The American

Act 3, Scene 1

[The voices contained herein are self-contained and non-differentiated, but are unique like crystals or fractals, which are neither unique nor practical. As you will find out, or have already surmised, Meta and The American were in love and somewhat obsessed with magic and the manifold dimensions of z. This final act, which isn't the final act, takes place in 2-space (film projection) and 3-space (live-action), which serve as parallel worlds that are unaware of the other, but are layered on top of each other like minks or foxes wearing stoles and fur coats. The characters are characters. The stage is a regal courthouse, and the lighting is still up to you, but don't overdo it.]

The American: Champagne, my Dear?

Meta: Yes, Dear.

The American: I'm not at all hungry, my Dear.

Meta: I am, my Dear.

The American: Will a pickle hold you over, my
                 Dear?

Meta: Yes, my Dear.

Scene 2

[The Boy, z, and negative z enter stage right, or left, or they are lowered from the rafters. The judges are minks and foxes wearing stoles, and the two boys are real boys insofar as two real complex coordinates on a graph can co-exist in the same space and at the same time. They are expertly illuminated (hire a real lighting director, please) and seated across from Meta and The American. The audience is like, whatever.]

Boy: z, do you feel the painful wounds of
                history in our genes?

z & -z: Boy, I'm not privy to things below the
                ionosphere. I'm tired, my little frog. I
                just want to go home.

Boy: Then why hang around?

z & -z: My wings are wet, slick as oil. I don't
                enjoy inclement weather.

Boy: Did you imagine an Egg would prosper
                into Big Bird?

z & -z: And find its way into the hands of noble
                humans.

Boy:	Who couldn't speak without cursing to Kingdom Come?
z & -z:	Fuck, ya'!
Boy:	z, with a little help, I think we can correct the polarity of the earth and bring you back to life.
z & -z:	It's possible, my friend, but the past is without solace.
Boy:	Slice me a pickle, then.

Scene 3

[z & -z, the Boy, Meta, and The American converse over each other in a Chrysler LeBaron Town & Country station wagon that is located left of center stage from the audience. The exterior of the wagon may or may not be wood paneled. The wagon also may or may not honk throughout the scene. All of the characters may or may not be visible to the others and the audience.]

The American:	Meta, dance with me. Come on, dance with me.
Meta:	I will only dance with the boy of my dreams, not you, nor little green men.
Boy:	z, are you the boy of her dreams?
z & -z:	Boy, I am the boy of our dreams.
Boy:	Be serious with me, man. Are you the boy of her dreams?
z & -z:	Boy, why did you decide to write little play plays?
Boy:	For sea lions and subatomic

things, whales and rubber dinghies. Impossible bees. Depth charges. And to tease.

z & -z: For the powers that be?

Boy: For the impossible swimming.

All: And for the cyclopedia of ancestry.

[The Boy speaks to the audience to rein them in, so to speak, and to give them a direct line into the psychosis of The Boy.]

Boy: Meta left us with gambling debts, worthless trinkets, and her dentures. She collected knick-knacks and things that went click-clack in the night.

z & -z: Do you still have the dress you wore to K-mart?

Boy: No, but I have her pocketbook, and the pink barrettes.

44

Scene 4

[This scene takes place just before Act 5 goes missing. Note: I am aware that something that is missing can't go missing until it's gone, like the boy who was lost (or will be lost again) in a future Act. Meta and The American are digging a grave in the desolate and frozen Danish landscape. The Chrysler LeBaron Town & Country station wagon is in the distance. There's a white pickup truck in the distance. It may or may not be a stolen vehicle.]

The American: Meta—(exclamation mark)

Meta: Yes, Billy.

The American: Meta—(exasperation mark)

Meta: What! Billy, what do you want?

The American: Marry me? Plea—

Meta: Not a fucking chance, Billy.

The American: Hold the shovel, Meta. I have to pee. It's Sunday.

Meta: I know, Billy. What do you mean?

The American: I have to pee. That's what I mean.

Meta: Sometimes I sit when I pee.

The American: Be serious, Meta. What do you mean?

Meta: Sometimes I pee when I think about z.

The American: When will you be done with this whole cartography? I'm tired of z.

Meta: When you stop digging, I will be done.

The American: Aren't his bones enough? This grave for two.

Meta: Billy, what is the nature of my cartography?

The American: My Dear, may I borrow your knuckles. I want bones to crush.

Meta: Here. My Dear, enjoy the weather.

[Sound of bones crushing.]

Scene 5

[This space is intentionally left speechless. Meta and The American are center stage shoveling black earth into an unremarkable grave. The audience can only hear what they are doing as they exit the theater for a brief intermission.]

Scene 6

[As it turns out, it is revealed in Scene 5 that Meta and The American bury the boy and his father, but there is room to grow, and the two didn't fail to use every inch of that grave. It is said before and will be said in this scene that Meta attempts one last act of resistance by converting action into language, or the metempsychosis of geometry. Elegant math equations are haphazardly projected against the background. There's one spotlight that shines on each character, who are all staged somewhere left of center stage. All else is black. Don't even think about removing Winnie the Pooh face down on the edge of center stage right.]

z & -z: Craps, just like the cartographer's map, is
            a vast gene pool of chance happenings.

Boy: None of the above, my Little z, will
            make sense to pelicans.

z & -z: I am a pelican.

Boy: And the scattered bones of my
            ancestors.

z & -z: The bones!

48

Boy: The bones!

z & -z: Of pelicans?

[Sound of bones crushing.]

z & -z: I didn't have a fucking chance, did I?

[Meta enters the body of the Boy and the projector projects documentary footage of Meta as a young woman entering Frøslev shortly after her capture. Her hair is shaved off. She holds her womb.]

Boy: Whole transports were women and
            children of all ages. It wasn't a circus or
            a gathering of angels. I saw alien species
            and spaceships filled with more aliens.

[The Boy reenters the body of the Boy.]

Boy: z & -z, listen to me.

[Meta reenters the body of the Boy as the documentary footage continues to flow above. Black Boots wielding rubber blackjacks enter the theater. They terrorize the audience. White Coats with German tongues enter the theater. In the film, White Coats hold Meta down against her will. They are about to remove her uterus when the film cuts out. The audience may or may not realize the significance of this particular kind of cruelty.]

Boy: It was the real deal, and there was nothing I could do to stop them. Not even swim. It was human behavior.

Boy: Hundreds of thousands of Billys fought against his manuscript. They crossed the border with the worst kind of sadomasochism.

[The audience whispers "sadomasochism" from the audience as the Black Boots cross the Danish border without meeting any resistance.]

Boy: Many of us climbed onto white busses with red crosses. They locked and loaded, aimed for our heads, but it was too late. It didn't matter what happened next. The watchmen uttered not a word, they didn't even whisper—not even Methuselah spoke.

[Methuselah enters stage left and enters the body of the Boy whose body is already occupied by Meta. The three of them—Methuselah, the Boy, and Meta—put on Meta's auburn wig with soft curls. Since they can't literally enter each other's body, they stand in a single

50

file line and each of the characters gently place the wig upon their heads. Methuselah first, Meta second, and the Boy third. They pucker and make fish faces as if they're looking in a mirror.]

z & -z: And then—?

Boy: I wish I hadn't seen with my own eyes
               how my own child was killed. I wish
               Billy would've dug and dug and dug
               and buried me with him down that
               fucking rabbit hole.

["Don't say fucking" the audience says. The light is on Methuselah, who transforms into Meta, but just for a moment.]

Meta: Fucking is how it felt.

[The couples in the audience now understand how it felt. You can see the flash of pain in their eyes.]

z & -z: And then—?

Boy: I wished upon a stone.
               I wished upon a firing squad.
               I wished for an assortment of magical
               wings.

51

Z: And then—?

Boy: With my own ears I heard the boy tiptoe
            off the ledge of something Big.

Z: You did.

Meta: I did.

Boy: It was the end.

Meta: It was the end.

[The audience is like, okay, we get it. If they don't, play
a dramatic orchestral number and drop the curtain.
There may or may not be another intermission.]

Coup de Grâce

Act 4, Scene 1

[Meta stages a coup backstage. Downstage the Boy, z, and -z continue their tête-à-tête while sitting on the same rock as Meta and the Boy. There's a light breeze blowing across the theater.]

z & -z   Boy, were you the archivist? The boy
              with two faces and elbow
              grease?

Boy: No. I'm not a fan of Grease, but I've
              always been in love with Olivia Newton
              John. I don't collect nor have the desire
              to claw through potash anymore.

z & -z: Then, why waste your breath?

Boy: For habeas corpus perhaps, or out of
              respect for cumulous nimbuses, or for
              Cyclops and his missing shoelaces.

z & -z   Are you obsessive compulsive?

Boy: About the past? Yes, who isn't?

-z   And about the boy called z, who was left
                alone (or abandoned to the wind) to roll
                boulders up icebergs until his death.

Boy: Until your death.

z & -z: Why waste your breath?

Boy: Because I can, because she left.

z & -z   "Meet me on the moon," she said to me
                before my last breath.

Boy: "In your dreams," she said to me before
                her last breath.

[From backstage.]

Meta: I love you, seismographs.

Act 5, Scene 1

[A poem by Meta read aloud while driving (north on I-95) and smoking with the windows rolled up in her Chrysler LeBaron Town & Country station wagon somewhere between the Orange Bowl and the Hollywood Sportatorium on or approximately near November 14th, 1981. The Boy is in the backseat trying to breathe.]

Meta: z,
I lost control of the weather.
[Honk, honk.]
In that moment it began to _ _ _ _.
(Inaudible.)
Billy was so afraid, and I was, too.
He dug and dug and dug, and it was so
cold we had to go,
but he broke through the ice,
and we buried your bones,
and the ice remained ice despite his
digging. Nothing could warm you up,
not even our hallelujahs or cuckoos.

You were so cold.
We were, too.

I filled your pea coat pockets with sand and
    stones just in case you wanted to breathe.
We lowered you feet first into the pigmented
    sea,
My little z,
(Meta, who is z?)
(Shut up and listen, kid!)
no one ever knew what was coming.

Scene 2

[The stage is black and empty. An audio recording plays. Winnie the Pooh remains in the same place. The Chrysler LeBaron Town & Country station wagon is mangled upstage. One headlight is on. The left blinker blinks.]

Voice Over: The police report that Meta was driving west on Sheridan Street when her car was broadsided by a pickup truck that was (heading) northbound on North 66th Avenue, Hollywood. She was on her way home from Jai-Alai.

[The dense fog may or may not dissipate at this point in the scene.]

Voice Over: Meta was in the Danish Underground Resistance and ended up in a concentration camp with other family members during World War II. She only spoke about it once to her daughter at Nami's a week before the accident.

[The dense fog may or may not continue to dissipate.]

Voice Over: Her husband, son, older brother, and other family members were all in the

resistance. She once told her daughter
Lillian that her experience in the camp
was too painful for her to talk about.
Almost no one made it out alive, except
for Meta and her sister.

[The audio recording crackles because that is what
makes the scene seem more real-real.]

Voice Over: "We met on a Sunday and were married
on Wednesday," The American said.
"She came (to the United States) in 1946
as a war bride."

[The dense fog is almost a mist.]

Voice Over: "We moved to Trenton, New Jersey
where we bought a diner that burned
down in a fire a year later. A year after
that when we decided to open a candy
shop with an old-fashioned soda
fountain in Jersey City. Meta ran a
sports betting racket out of the
backroom."

[The fog is almost entirely gone.]

Voice Over:	Before they moved to Florida, Meta & The American adopted a baby girl on February 5th, 1949. She was born with spinal meningitis and wasn't expected to live. They named her Lillian.

[Two voices emerge from the dark, and they are having a telephone conversation.]

The Boy:	Hi.
The American:	She didn't have a chance.
The Boy:	That's enough.
The American:	The driver was drunk and ran this or that.
The Boy:	That's enough, I said. I have to pee. Talk to you later.

[The Boy hangs up.]

Scene 3

[Meta and Lillian sit next to each other at the hibachi grill in Nami's Japanese Restaurant. Two iced teas and a California roll are in front of them. The stage is black except for a single spotlight cast upon Meta & Lillian, the hibachi grill, and the hibachi chef. 90s music plays in the background. The Chrysler LeBaron Town & Country station wagon is parked near the entrance to the restaurant. The headlights are on.]

She said: I swept the bloody streets of Copenhagen and gave them the finger. I planned my escape with a Virgo inside my tummy—or was he holding my hand? I can't remember.

You asked: What else do you remember?

She said: I can't remember. Anything.

You asked: What were their names?

She said: Anyway and Always.

You asked: What else do you remember?

She said: I understood the politics of sex during

war. The knife to the throat. I confessed
to no one, not even goats. I always
carried a bag of tobacco, dried herring,
diary, pencil, cyanide pill, vitamins,
postage, a small knife, and such things
that could be useful when the time
came, like watches, penicillin, gold,
another small knife, garter belt

—and my little ragamuffin.

You asked: What was his name?

She said: When the time came, I lost his name.
The boy is the map. I had no direction
after him. The Black Boots snatched him
and made me beg for his life. On my
knees. Always holding my hand.

You asked: Then what?

She said: They killed Anyway.

You asked: What was his name?

She said: Anyway, with his hand in my hand.

You asked: What was his name?

She said: I placed my womb around my arm.

You said: You mean you placed your arm around your womb.

She said: My womb around my arm.

You asked: Then, what?

She said: I kicked the bastards in the shins. I ran, but it was too late. Anyway and Always. They were no more or less. There was nothing left to remember. I don't remember their names.

[The hibachi chef lights the onion volcano. Meta jumps. Her iced-tea spills across the hibachi grill and sizzles.]

You asked: I'm sorry. Please, sit down.

She said: They punched my lights out, and I woke up in Frøslev. (Pause 3 seconds.) Like this.

You asked: Like what?

She said: [Raises her hands up in the air.]

You asked: [Lillian hands Meta a sepia

62

photograph.] Do you remember their
names?

She said: In one photograph exists an entire
person and the next generation—just as
in one sliver of the night sky exists a
billion galaxies engaged in an infinite
dance of the death spiral.

You asked: I'm sorry for what they did to you.

She said: I will always remember where I came
from.

You said: I will remember, too.

She said: Never tell your children what I've done.

Part 3 | Rigsarkivet

The Danish National Archives (Rigsarkivet)

Subj: Danish Resistance

Date: 8/9/2002 10:25:11 AM Eastern Standard Time
From: ███████████████████████████
To: ███████████████████

Thank you very much for your email and your requests. I have searched our resources and I have found some websites which may prove to be useful in your search and also please remember that you are always welcome to look up our website www.denmarkemb.org should you wish to gather information on Denmark. With regard to your specific request on information on the resistance in Denmark, I have found the following addresses which may be able to help you further:

Rigsarkivet
Rigsdagsgården 9
DK- 1218 Copenhagen K
www.as.dk/ra
email: ████████████████████

www.frihedsmuseet.dj/sw73.asp - from this website

you can send a message with your question to the museum.

Also, I found two gentlemen who did a project on the resistance in Denmark, and they may be able to help you with some links to where you can find more information. Their email address from the website is: ████████████████

Finally, I have this link where you can perhaps trace your Danish roots.

www.migrationinstitution.fi/nordic

I hope that the above information will be useful in your search. Please feel free to contact me should you have any questions in the future.

Kind regards,
████████████████
Administrative Officer

Subj: Danish Resistance

Date: 8/9/2002 1:45:10 PM Eastern Standard Time
From:
To:

I have checked the websites and as you correctly
indicate I could not connect to the websites. However,
I have typed it again and when I type it I can connect.
Please find the following internet address which is
certainly working: www.migrationinstitute.fi/nordic

Furthermore, I have found the address for the Danish
Emigration Archives www.emiarch.dk/arc.php3?l=da
which you may be able to use. Perhaps you can
contact them in order to find out about the permit you
mention in your email.

I wish you all the best with your research and your
book and I hope that you can use the information I
have given you.

Kind regards,
Linda Hansen

Subj: Danish Resistance

Date: 8/30/2002 5:11:32 AM Eastern Standard Time
From: █████████████████████████
To: ██████████████████████

The National Archives have received your email of
August 27th. 2002 concerning the Danish Resistance
and Meta's role in the resistance. To find information
about private persons in the archives, it is necessary
for us to have her name and day of birth. Then we can
examine the archives of the Danish authorities to find
cases concerning her.

Most documents from the German occupation of
Denmark are still closed, and you will need a
permission of access to see the files. Concerning
general information about the German occupation of
Denmark, the National Archives can recommend you
to consulate printed books at a public library.

Yours sincerely
███████████████████
Arkivfuldmægtig

Subj: **Danish Resistance**

Date: 9/10/2002 8:03:36 AM Eastern Standard Time
From: ██████████████████████████████████
To: ████████████████████████

In reply to your email of August, 16 2002 concerning
Meta Alvilda Lorenzen Hansen, born December 13,
1922, The Danish National Archives (Rigsarkivet) can
tell you that we have no information about her
participation in the Danish Resistance against the
German occupation. We have investigated the files of
the Attorney General of Special affairs, without any
result. We can recommend you ask The Danish
Museum of Resistance (Frihedsmuseet).

The address is Churchillparken, 1263 København K..
E-Mail: ███████████████████████████████

Sincerely Yours,
███████████████████

arkivfuldmægtig
Publ. Dept.

Date: 9/11/2002 2:49:03 AM Eastern Standard Time
From: ████████████████████████
To: ██████████████████████████████

Yes, we have some records from some few Danish Concentration camps (Horserød og Frøslev); but the records are not complete. They are written in Danish, and you need an access of permission to get them. If you will obtain an access of permission, you have to write a formal application.

Sincerely Yours,
████████████████████
Publ.Dept.

Subj: Danish Resistance

Date: 9/19/2002 7:17:02 AM Eastern Standard Time
From: ██████████████████████████████████
To: ████████████████████████████████

Yes, you have to write a real letter with your request and with the purpose of your investigation. And please, tell us your address.

Sincerely Yours,

████████████████

Date: 10/19, 2002, at 6:03 AM Eastern Standard Time
From: █████████████████████████████
To: ██████████████████████████████████

We might have some information about Meta in our
archives, we do, however, need her personal data in
order to find out. So, please send these!

Sincerely,
███████████████████████████

Overinspektør/Head of Department
NATIONALMUSEET/THE NATIONAL MUSEUM
OF DENMARK
Frøslevlejrens Museum/The Froslev Camp Museum
www.natmus.dk

Subj: Danish Resistance

Date: 10/24, 2002, at 5:03 PM Eastern Standard Time
From: ████████████████████████████
To: ████████████████████████

We have no record of Meta, her sister, Lilly ████████
(or Lilly ██████████), or her husband, or her son.
However, our records are incomplete. I apologize for
this. I know the photographs are all that you have.

Sincerely,
███████████████████████████
Overinspektør/Head of Department
NATIONALMUSEET/THE NATIONAL MUSEUM
OF DENMARK
Frøslevlejrens Museum/The Froslev Camp Museum
www.natmus.dk

Epilogue

You: Are you the bear of logic?

& I: I am the bear with the xed out eyes, the
            see-through stomach, and the astronaut
            suit. I would swear instead, but
            lumberjacks wouldn't understand the
            grrrr of bear behavior, especially in the
            light of the half-lit moon while staring
            down the barrel of a gun. I apologize for
            my use of poetic mumbo jumbo and
            cliché, but I'm Icelandic in the sense I
            come from ice and sex.

You: How can you come from ice and sex?

& I: Cosmological sediments, of sorts. Or
            maybe I just wish I came from ice and
            sex, the cosmo-genetic offspring of
            hydrogen and oxygen. Or maybe, just
            maybe, I am truly Icelandic in the sense
            I roam the land of ice.

You: Are you sure?

& I: No, but I'm a bear.

You: As you were.

& I: As I was, or were, I am entitled to

artifice.

You: Why?

& I: You see, I don't want to be the
            stereotypical bear anymore, the one
            with my very own Discovery Channel
            show and make-up crew. Save the
            planet is for Greenpeace. I don't mind
            representing my race but, you see, I just
            want to be ice. Do my part to fight the
            global boring (chuckles).

You: Bear, you are heading off topic.

& I: I even wonder what bears would taste
            like in a human's mouth, or what a bear
            would taste like to water.

You: What the—

& I: Water is just as good as ice, but I revel in
            the inextricable consequence of
            consumption—

You: Please, don't say it—

& I: Water goes in then comes out.
            Reincarnation, something you

humans haven't been able to achieve yet
with your almighty gods and fathers
almighty.

You: What were you looking for in the
                tunnel?

& I: Logic. A spoon. A little Bjork.

You: I get the sense your identity is
                somewhat stereoscopic. Do you
                ever get confused?

& I: All we are is all we all are.

You: In other words?

& I: You see that's the thing about bear
                behavior. We act beyond
                language. We're human entertainment
                systems without remote control, yet we
                are really mirror-mirrors.

You: On the wall?

& I: This tête-à-tête is going nowhere.

You: Patience my bear, listen. If you are a
                bear and I am a human, then what are

we in retrospect? In other words, if you
= x, and I = y, then why z?

& I: Because you have to have difference to
            see no difference.

You: Do you ever feel like an alien?

& I: Like never before.

You: Are you moody?

& I: Only when the weather is warm.

You: What's your relationship with
            elephants?

& I: They're anti-bear with a nose of terror
            just like a lumberjack with
            his shotgun.

You: Are you afraid of anything?

& I: The fact love is a 4-letter word.

You: Why are lumberjacks drawn to the
            light?

& I: Because they are drawn to it.

82

You: Are you moody?

& I: As never before.

You: Is it true that you are not a real bear, but
          a girl in a costume or a
          boy inside a boy?

& I: Is it true you are a man in a costume
          dressed as a woman?

You: Answer the question.

& I: That's the thing with you guys. You
          always try to blame it on Little Red
          Riding Hood or Dorothy or the little gay
          boy or the pre-goth-emo child dressed
          in black or the Iraqi dentist who just
          wants to fix teeth and get married.

You: Are you really a girl? Answer the
          question.

[The lumberjack locks and loads as the bear locks and
loads.]

& I: Even if I am a real girl, I am just as
          artificial as you.

83

You: Do you love me?

& I: Whenever you think about me.

Acknowledgements

"Minkowskian Spacetime: The Geometry of Meta,"
  Dogzplot

"The Archivist," *kill author*

"The Ars Magna For The Manifold Dimensions of z ,"
  Pank

"The Manifold Dimensions of z" (as "Methuselah's
  Voice Over." *Fringe*

Multiple publications in *The Offending Adam*:
"When Kids Get Too Much Information About a
  Chance Meeting"
"Upon Recovering from Too Much Information"
"When I Was Nineteen"
"When They Ate, They Made Love"
"Terrified & Wigless"
"On the Futility of Digging"
"In Medias Res/istance"
"Chocolate Doesn't Help"
"On the Military Underground Resistance" (as "Vireo
  Gilvus")

JACKLEG PRESS

Other Titles

jacklegpress.org

CPSIA information can be obtained
at www.ICGtesting.com
Printed in the USA
BVHW081536211021
619555BV00007B/241

9 781737 330745